Poets Wear Boots

1990 - 2020

Lou Sceelo

Artwork by Theodore Rodriguez

Poets Wear Boots

Paperback Edition

ISBN (978-0-578-23466-3)

Printed in USA

DEDICATION

For Theo

PREFACE

This book took 30 years to complete. What you have in your hands are original works begun in 1990 as lyrics to a post-punk rock band called The Vivians. I always felt my lyrics stood up like poetry and that perhaps one day I'd publish them. And here we are. The artwork was all done by my beautiful and talented son Theo. I hope you enjoy this book and keep it for years to come.

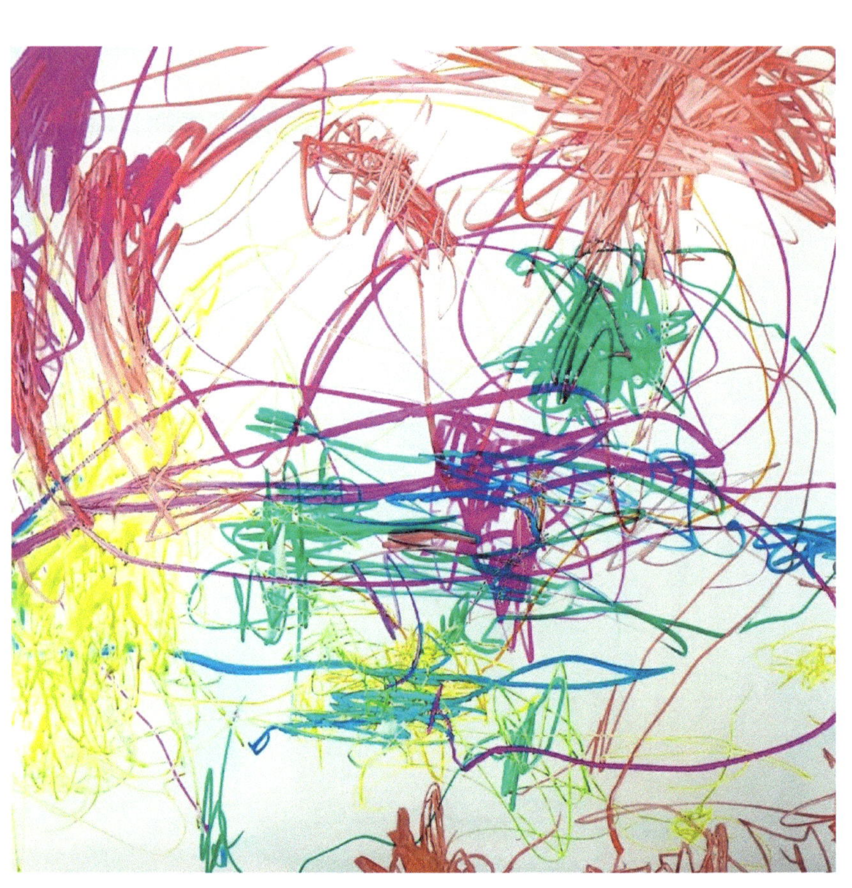

The Bee Charmers

Idle smiles
on so many
fools faces
longing for pleasure
but now you must
settle here
it's not the time and place
to tell you my dear
some are plagued
with restless jealousy
The Bee Charmers
dearest don't you delay me
be there soon
for time hasn't been there
for us
I ever must
complain oh time
with its craft and cruel cunning
time hasn't been there for us
The Bee Charmers
secret flower
full-blown
dead in an hour
have I been there for you?
you have charmed me
an inch from my life
Oh the Bee Charmers
Idle smiles
on so many
fools faces
longing for pleasure
but now you must
settle here
many are plagued
with restless jealousy
you don't even know why
but i'm trying to
see you through

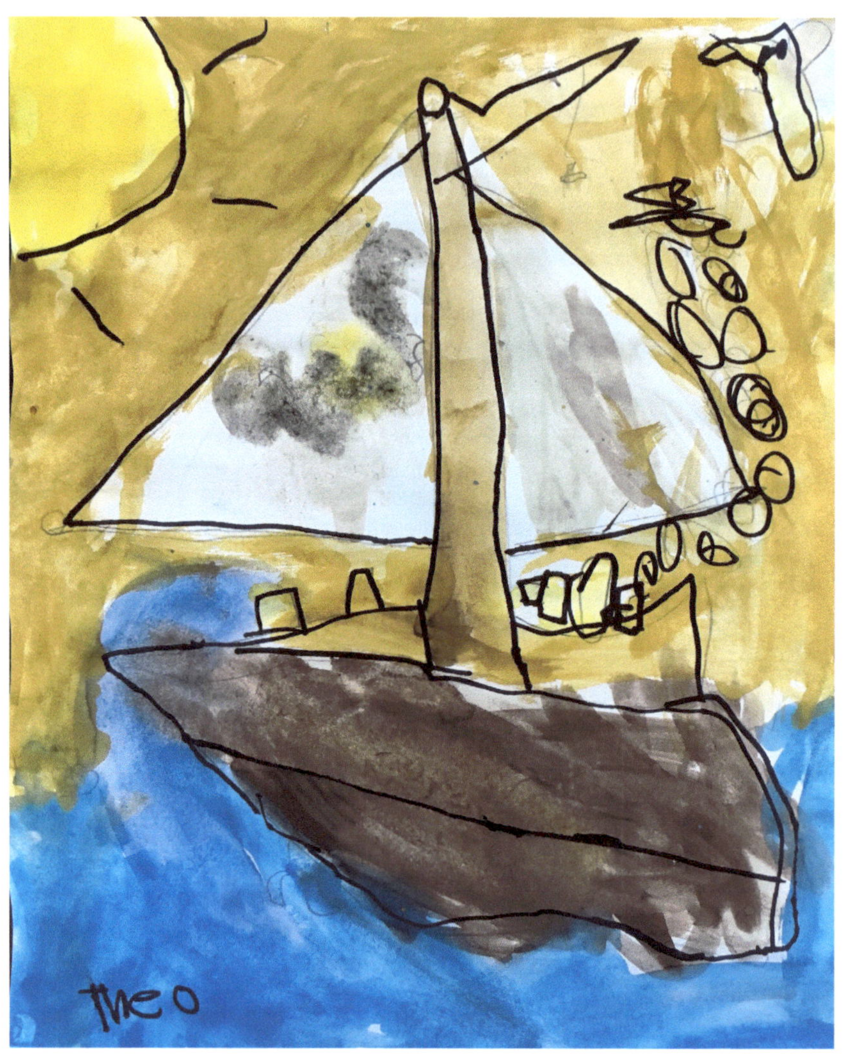
theo

Sun Sets In

Sun sets in
we both know why we're here
Sun sets in
we both know what we want
Come over here
I want you near
You must not refuse
You must not back away
We must not hide
our feelings
we both know why we're here
we both know what we want
Yet you still prolong
The days are not for us
to take so calm
Oh you must not refuse
No you must not back away
I'm here and ready
so take me far away
Sun sets in
we both know why we're here
Sun sets in
we both know what we want
Come over here
I want you near
You must not refuse
You mustn't back away
You must not hide
your feelings
Are there any?

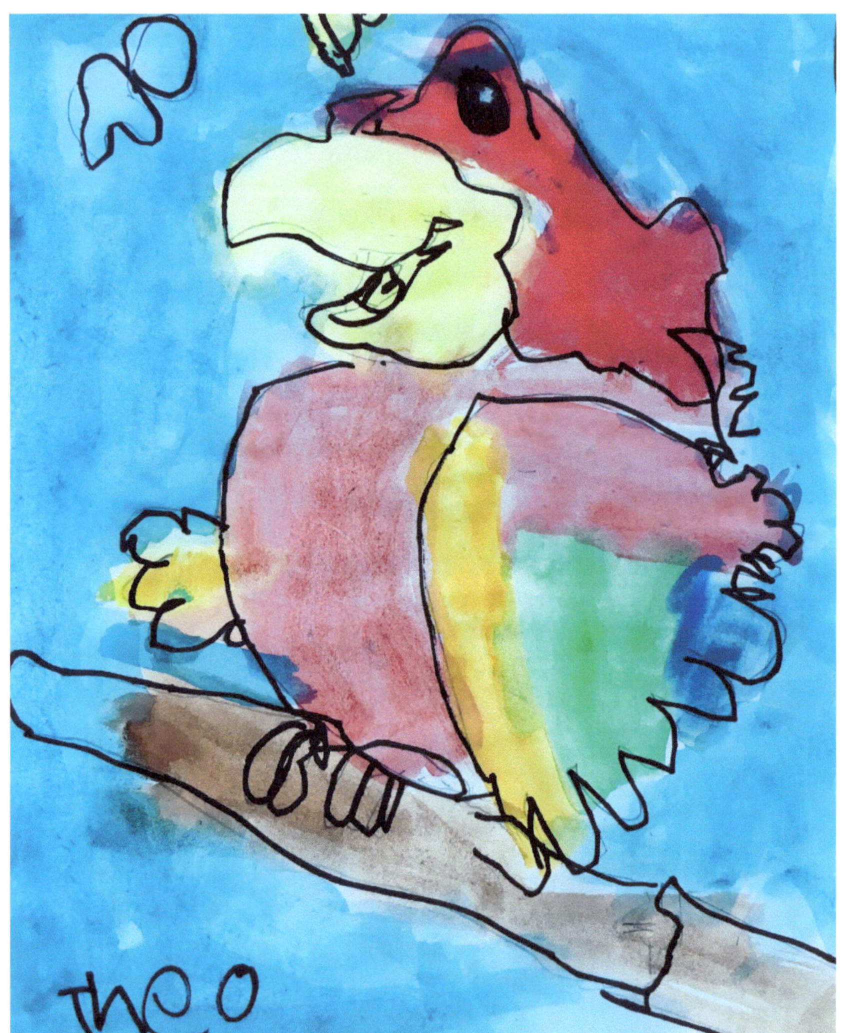
theo

CASUAL CRUELTY

SHIMMY SHIMMY SHIMMY BY
THE CLOUDS ROLL IN
AND MAKE A RIPPLING SKY

YOU BURY YOURSELF
IN YOUR SOFA AND SAY:
"OH SHE'S THE ONE FOR ME
AND I'LL LOVE HER TILL THE
DAY I DIE"

THERE SHE GOES
NOT FAR AWAY
SHE'LL STEAL YOUR HEART
THEN LEAD YOU ASTRAY

AND AS THE WIND
RATTLES THE CHIME
YOU REALIZE SHE PLAYED TRICKS
ON YOUR HEART AND MIND:
"OH WHERE'S THE SLIMMER
OF HUMAN COMPASSION?
SHE'S JUST PART OF
HEARTLESS FASHION"

THERE SHE GOES
HER VERY OWN WAY
TIPPING HER HAT
AS SHE LEAD YOU ASTRAY

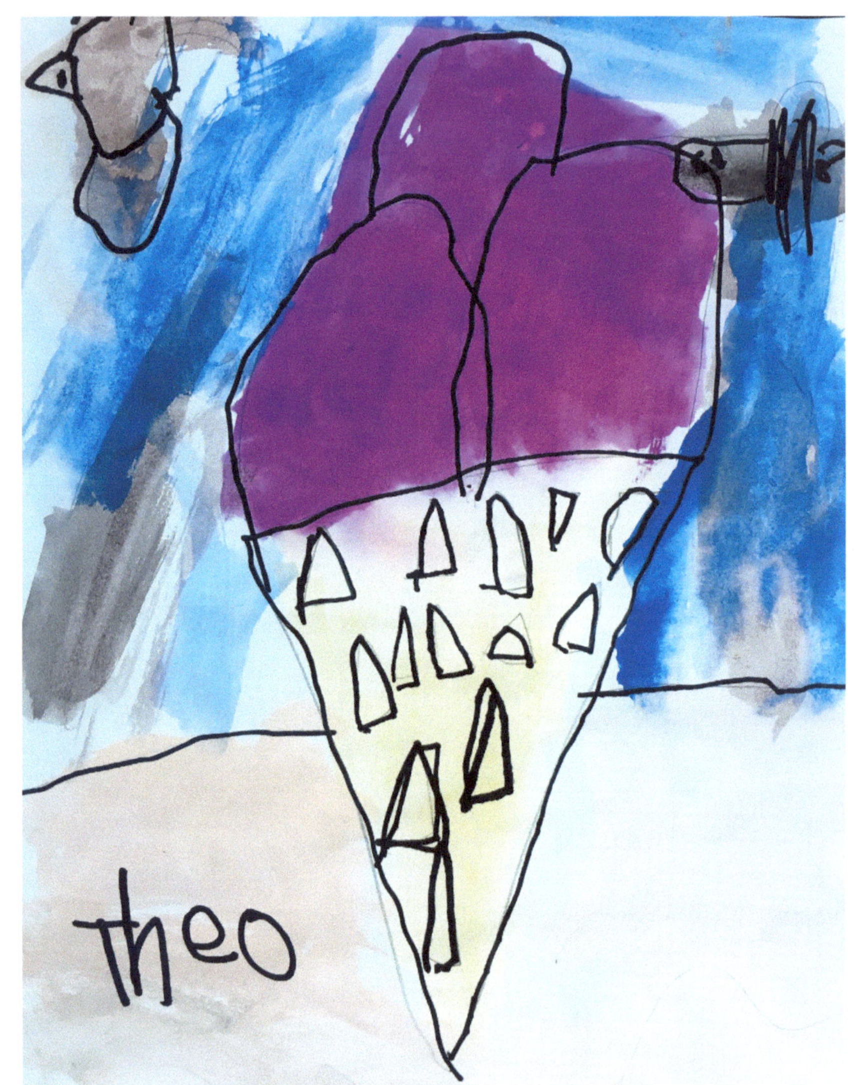
theo

Interlude

So smiles the spring
So shines the sun
For a lovely lull
Has come undone
Don't save your voice
What need we else
Beauty like the sun
Does shine
Hymns devout
Your too true words
Cast such a clout
So don't save your voice
What need we else?
The kind and true are
well defined
Yes, the kind and true are
well inclined
Now the lovely lull
Has come and gone
As quick a growth
To meet decay
All too soon
I heard you say:
"Sing Sing Sing along
to these drowsy words
of desire, Come let us sing
till the lonely days expire"

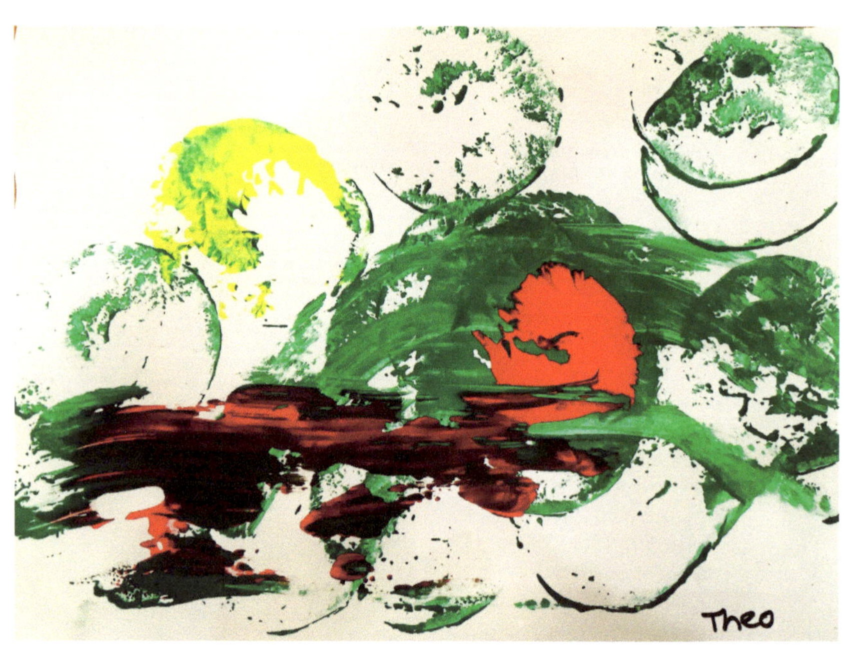
Theo

Twice Was Enough

I got a gun
let me go
I got a gun
let me go
gonna shoot my fate
straight in the heart
you know you know
I tried so long
to help you
but no
now the months
gain on you
and me
there you go
I see you now
but I don't want you
anymore
I just don't want you
anymore
tried so hard for you
all I got was a closed door
twice was enough for me
you see
you didn't want me
the dream will always live
with me
I leaped like a
performing flea
closed door
you didn't want to hear from me

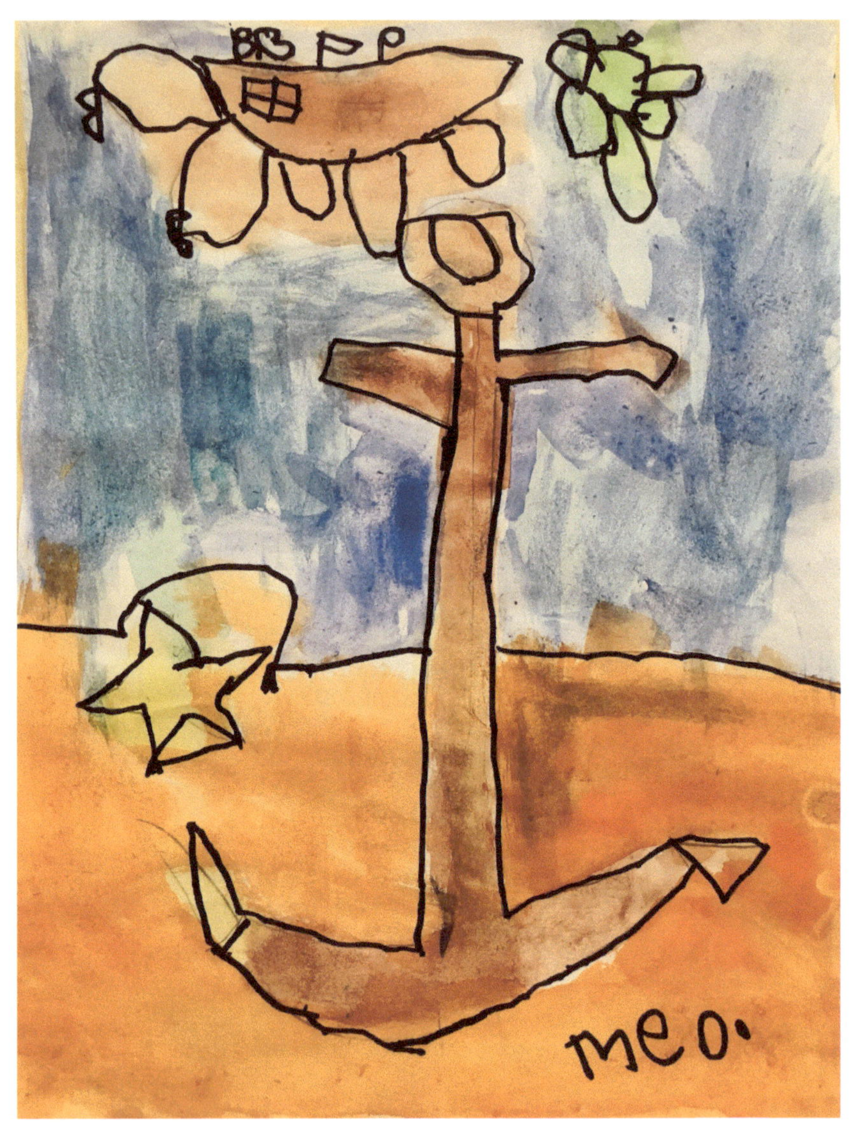
meo.

THE PRIZE IDIOT

The PRIZE idiot is
coming my way
I CAN'T See him
BUT CAN hear him
AND don't UNderstAND
what he's tRYING to SAY
- JUST don't GET in his WAY
"You're Lonely But you have
A FREE LIFE"
Is it tRUE that
the Shores ARE LONLIER
AND the waters more deepen
where I'm going AND
COMING FROM?
OH YES
I Fill my empty weekends
tAKING SNApshots

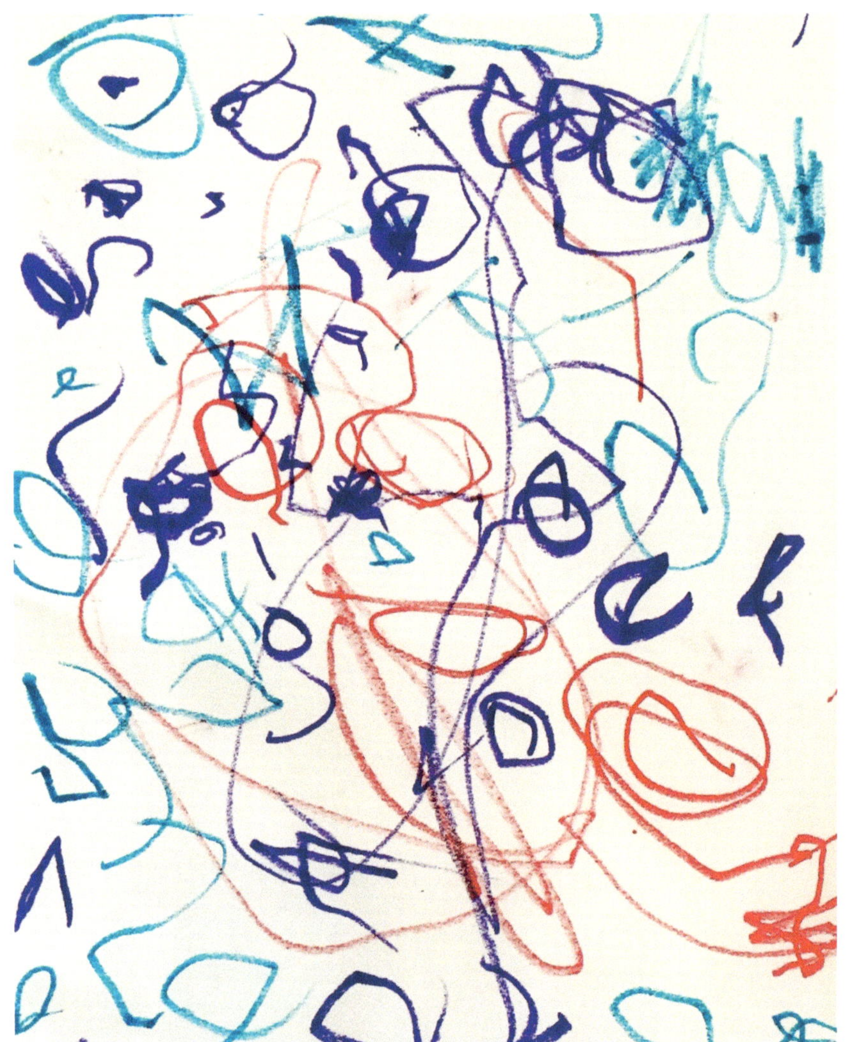

The Laughing Listeners

No one here is likely
to believe in you
Now that you're gone
chances are they'll
lap it up
Who is she
lovely as the day is long
traveling all around
causing so many heads
to turn her way
My canny dowager
Skies above
and Earth down below
can't give me a reason
to decide to let her go
The Laughing Listeners
standing all around her
only want to see her choke
hide her head
and have to
run away
My canny dowager
My canny dowager
No one here was likely
to believe in you
oh but I do
and chances are
they'll grasp it too
The Laughing Listeners
standing all around her
only want to see her choke
hide her head
and have to
run away

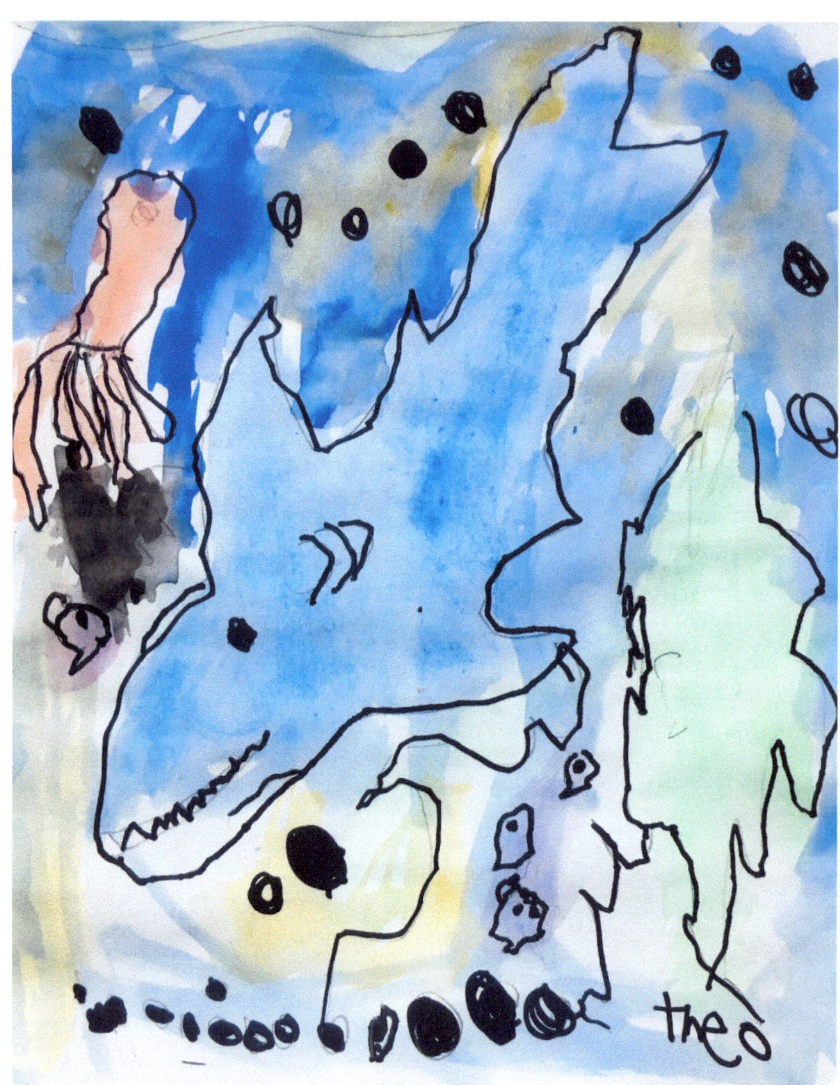
theo

Cruel Eyes

Turn away
those cruel eyes
Like the ones on some
perfumed guy
Knowing nothing of
the real world
Simply talking and living
and being free
A woman fades away
as everything with time does
such a sad reality
Knowing nothing of
the real world
Simply talking and living
and being free
Sparkling with red-orange flames
My heart and soul
once had names
I see and feel and I think
there must be more to life than this
Turn away
those cruel eyes
Like the ones on some
perfumed guy
I see and feel and I think
there must be more to life than this

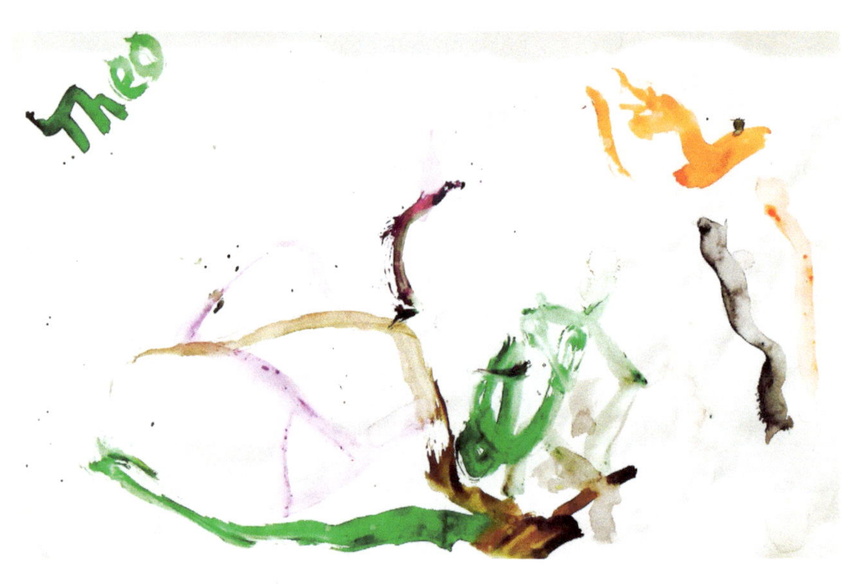
Theo

Surface Charm

Oh you
old and august
a missing
consoling presence
this is
surface charm
it's no harm
it's just
surface charm
where everyone
is nice
it's no harm
bow here
bow there
it's all good
it's surface charm
it never ends
we come thin-lipped
with surface charm
oh it's all good
there's no harm
this is just
surface charm

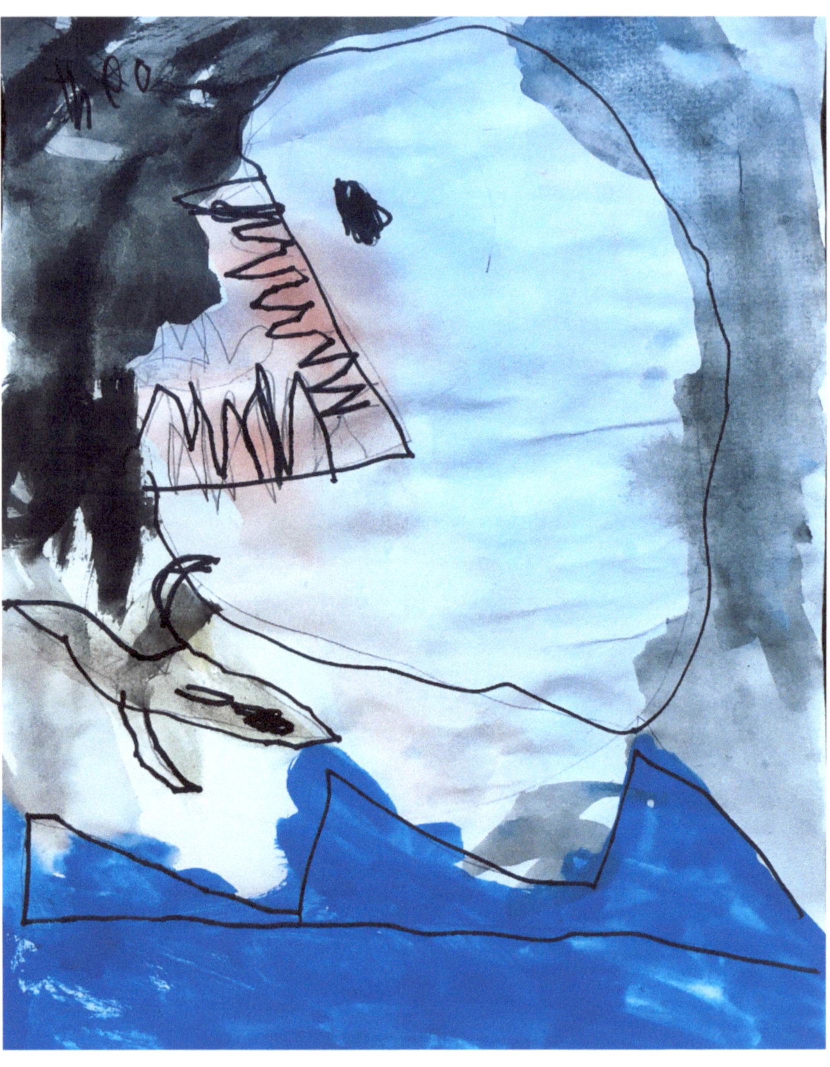
theo

The Rivers Bend

See you by the river bend
but I don't know if you're real
Sitting there cross-legged
worrying more about your gums
Oh it scares me why
we can't meet here and now
oh please
See I've waited oh so long
I really want this to be real
oh please
See you by the river bend
but I don't know if you're real
I see I feel I think
this could be real happiness
Hope you can hear me clearly
from down below as I call your name
so loudly
I see I feel I think I know
that you'll like me
So grab your bags
take my hand
and we'll stride away
from here
See you by the river bend
but I don't know how long I can wait
See you by the river bend
but I want you here by me
I see I feel I think I know
that it is time to go to go to go
I see I feel I think I know
that you'll be next to me

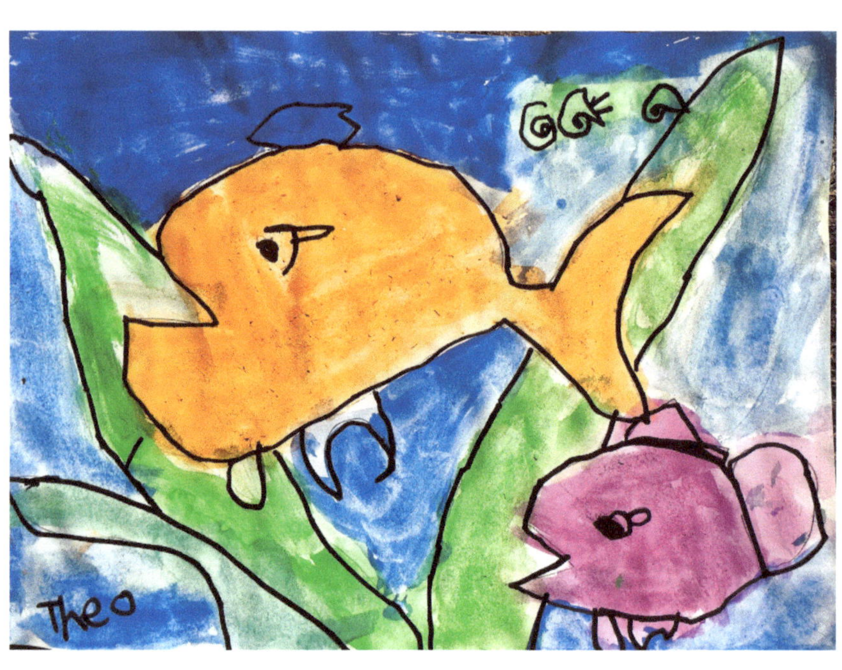
Theo

Seek and Find

go forth
seek and find
for heaven knows
you've been too kind
the world
is an ocean
deep hue
deepest blue
don't swim in circles
or stay on top
go deep
seek and find
take a bite
out of life

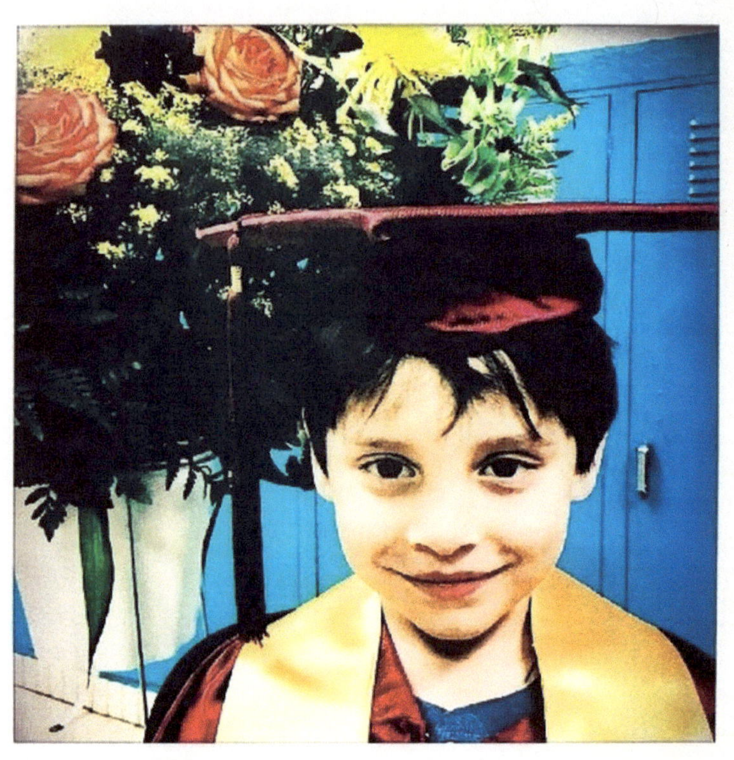

~KINDERGARTEN~
CLASS OF 2019

Teo

ese niño
tan chiquito
tan bonito
se llama teo
es un niño
muy bonito
muy chiquito
se llama teo
la da da da
la da da da
la da da da
la da da da
es precioso
y gracioso
ese niño
tan chiquito
tan bonito
se llama teo
lo quiero mucho
mucho mucho
a mi niño
ese Teo

www.ingramcontent.com/pod-product-compliance
Lightning Source LLC
LaVergne TN
LVHW052303100826
845147LV00001B/123

* 9 7 8 0 5 7 8 2 3 4 6 6 3 *